A BEGINNER'S GUIDE TO
KUMIHIMO

First published in Great Britain 2018
Search Press Limited
Wellwood, North Farm Road,
Tunbridge Wells, Kent TN2 3DR

Reprinted 2019

Text copyright © Donna McKean-Smith
Photographs by Paul Bricknell at Search Press Studios
Photographs and design copyright
© Search Press Ltd 2018

ISBN: 978-1-78221-534-9

The Publishers and author can accept no responsibility
for any consequences arising from the information,
advice or instructions given in this publication.

Publishers' note
You are invited to visit the author's website at
www.riversidebeads.co.uk

Suppliers
If you have difficulty in obtaining any of the materials
and equipment mentioned in this book, then please
visit the Search Press website for details of suppliers:
www.searchpress.com

All the step-by-step photographs in this book feature
the author, Donna McKean-Smith, demonstrating
how to make kumihimo jewellery. No models have
been used.

Dedication

To the Scroby ladies – love you all. #alwaysapride
     To my husband, Steve, and wonderful boys, Alex,
Kyle and Zack, for giving me the time and support
while I wrote this book. May your lives give you
endless opportunities to do the things you love.

Acknowledgements

To my customers: I thank you for your part in my
journey and your continuous support.
     To the wonderful Riverside team for their passion
and hard work.
     To Search Press for the opportunity to share my
love of beading.
     Happy braiding!

A BEGINNER'S GUIDE TO
KUMIHIMO

12 beautiful braided jewellery projects to get you started

Donna McKean-Smith

SEARCH PRESS

CONTENTS

INTRODUCTION

CRAFTING AND JEWELLERY-MAKING
have been passions of mine from an early age. I was
instantly hooked when I first discovered kumihimo and
saw the many variations of braids that can be created.
All you need to create your own kumihimo jewellery is
a basic starter kit, enthusiasm and the knowledge that this
book will give you.
I have designed the projects in this book with beginners
in mind, so no prior knowledge is required. I hope this
book will also help you to progress your braiding with
some of the design variations I have included.
Kumihimo is a portable craft that can be enjoyed
anywhere, by people of all ages. You will soon be making
your own beautiful braided and beaded kumihimo pieces.

Happy braiding!

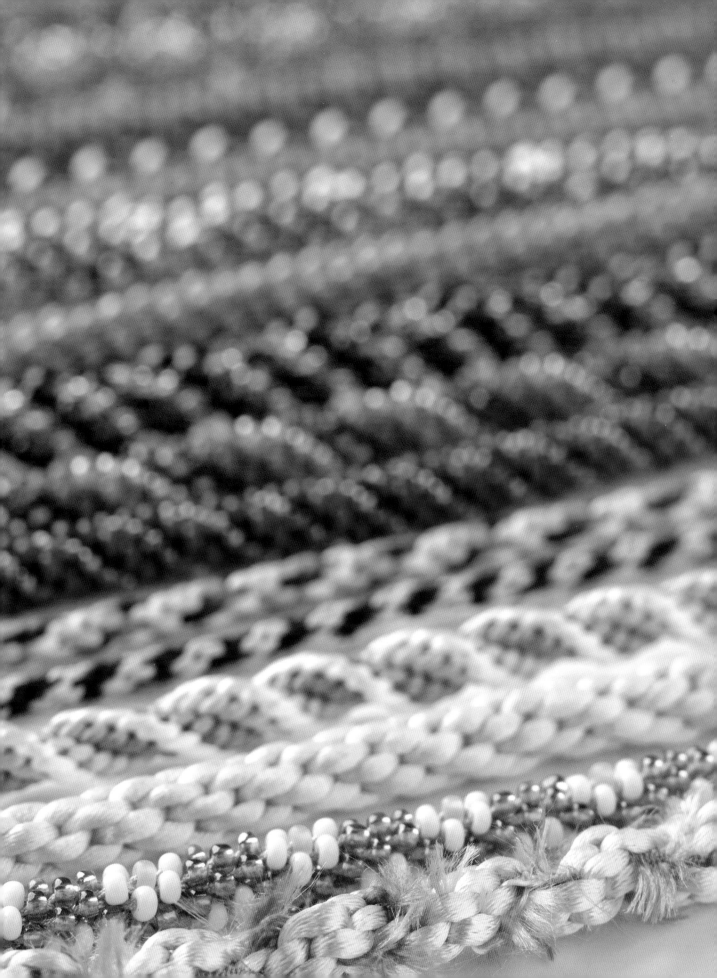

MATERIALS

You need only a few materials to get started with this wonderful craft, and to create beautiful projects. Kumihimo discs are lightweight and portable, making kumihimo braiding the perfect craft for taking out and about.
You will be able to buy all the materials you need for your kumihimo projects from a craft shop.

KUMIHIMO DISCS

There are a few different kumihimo discs available, including circular discs in two standard sizes – the larger disc shown on the right, below, is 15cm (6in) in diameter; the smaller disc is 11cm (4¼in) in diameter. Discs come in different thicknesses and even shapes – including the square plate, shown on the left of the photograph. The square plate can be used to create flat braids.

To create the braids demonstrated in this book, you can use either a large or small circular disc – for most projects I have used the larger disc but the braid size will be the same regardless of the disc size.

BOBBINS

Use bobbins to help prevent your cord or beads from tangling. Bobbins are particularly useful for longer projects such as necklaces, as you will have more loose cord under the disc that may get in the way while you are braiding.

Clockwise, from top left: a square kumihimo plate, large circular disc, a collection of bobbins, and a small circular disc.

Top row, from left: wire, 0.6mm macramé cord (two reels), 1mm satin cord, 2mm satin cord; middle row: beading thread (Nymo, two reels); S-Lon (three reels); bottom row: ribbon in teal and purple; textured fibre.

CORDS AND THREADS

SATIN (OR RAT-TAIL) CORD

Satin cord is typically available in thicknesses of between 1–2mm. The size of your cord determines the diameter of your finished braid; therefore the larger the cord, the wider your finished braid will be.

S-LON AND MACRAMÉ CORD

0.5mm S-Lon (Tex 210) and 0.6mm macramé cord are two perfect cords for your beaded kumihimo projects: they are strong and flexible and, when prepared correctly, the beads will fit on with ease. You can also use both cords to braid on their own, giving a fine finished braid.

OTHER BRAIDABLE MATERIALS

You can use your kumihimo disc to braid with ribbon, leather and even wire. You may find that if you work with different materials – especially wire – you may need more than one disc for each of the materials.

BEADING THREAD

Use a beading thread such as Nymo to whip around, and secure, the ends of your finished piece (see page 16).

BEADS

A wide variety of beads can be used on your kumihimo projects to create unique and stylish designs. Seed beads of assorted sizes are popular for beaded braids; however, the fantastic selection of shapes and types of beads available will allow you to develop your braiding skills and create some wonderfully varied designs.

END CAPS, FINDINGS, BUTTONS AND CHARMS

End caps are available in a variety of sizes and types: some have an extension chain and clasp, others simply have a hole at one end, so that you can attach the cap to the end of a bag charm, or a bookmark, where a clasp is not required. Magnetic end caps are also available: these are perfect for using on bracelets that might prove difficult to fasten – see *Maxine*, the eight-braid cuff project, on pages 62–67.

Buttons can be used as an alternative way to fasten your bracelets – such as for *Loraine*, the 'inside-out' bracelet on pages 34–37.

ADDITIONAL MATERIALS

WEIGHTS

A weight can be used to pull the centre of the braid down through the hole in the disc (see page 15). You can make your own weight using a selection of heavy glass beads and a clasp, as shown here, top left.

BEADING NEEDLES AND EMBROIDERY SCISSORS

A good pair of embroidery scissors is essential for cutting and preparing your cord before threading on any beads.

You will need a beading needle for *Maxine*, the eight-braid cuff project on pages 62–67.

BEADING MAT

A beading mat is a great purchase as its textured surface prevents your beads rolling about as you attempt to load them onto your needle or beading thread. Beading mats are available in assorted sizes and colours.

GLUE

To secure your braid into your end cap (see page 17), it is advisable to use a good, strong glue that is suitable for use with metal and fabric, and will dry clear, with flexibility when the piece is worn. E6000 and Zap Glue – both strong crafting adhesives – are two of the most popular brands for this purpose; however, if you are in need of quicker-drying glue, a cement glue such as Hypo, or a two-part epoxy glue may be better.

CLEAR NAIL POLISH

An item many of us have in our cupboards – use nail polish to prepare and stiffen the ends of your cord before you thread on your beads (see page 18).

TAPE MEASURE OR RULER

Either of these tools is useful for measuring wrist size and braid length.

ESSENTIAL TECHNIQUES

Kumihimo braids are created by taking the cord from underneath the disc and moving to another position on the disc. If you are a newcomer to kumihimo, I recommend that you make a braided eight-braid bracelet first, in order to become familiar with the repetition of moving the cords and how they sit on the disc. You can then progress to the more complex projects later in the book to develop your skills. This technique can be applied to many of the projects in this book.

WHAT IS EIGHT-BRAID?

Eight-braid is the most straightforward method of kumihimo braiding, involving – as the name suggests – eight strands of cord, or braids, that are moved around the disc in a particular sequence of movements. Most of the projects in this book use eight braids, but I have included projects that use seven, or twelve, braids as well – the number of cords you use, and the way you move them on the disc bring about a variety of design possibilities.

MEASURING YOUR CORD

The amount of cord you will need for each individual bracelet project will depend on the thickness of the cord and the pattern you are following.

For eight-braid bracelets, you can generally determine the length of your finished piece by wrapping the cord around your wrist, taking the circumference measurement, then multiplying that measurement by four to calculate the length of cord required.

As an example, for a 17¾cm (7in)-long eight-braid bracelet, measure 72cm (28¼in) of cord. I recommend that you then add another 10–20cm (4–8in) onto the length of each cord to ensure that you do not run out, as you will not be able to add cord onto your project at any stage during the braiding process. You will need to cut four pieces of cord of equal length.

You can also determine the approximate diameter of the finished braid by twisting together the number of strands of cord you are using together – for example, for a standard eight-braid twist, take the eight strands (four cords, folded in half) and twist them together to get a idea of the finished braid size.

tip

Bear in mind that any clasps you wish to add to your braid once complete will add up to 2.5cm (1in) to the length of your completed piece.

NOTE

With the exception of *Maxine*, the eight-braid cuff (see pages 62–67), the cord lengths given for each project will make a bracelet that is approximately 17¾cm (7in) in length. You can use the techniques on this page to get a more accurate measurement of cord for the length of bracelet you require.

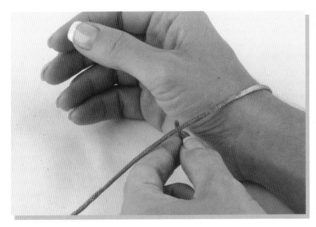

1 Wrap the cord around your wrist to measure the length (circumference) of the finished piece.

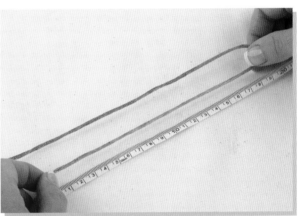

2 Measure the cord from your wrist and multiply the length by four. Add on an extra 10–20cm (4–8in).

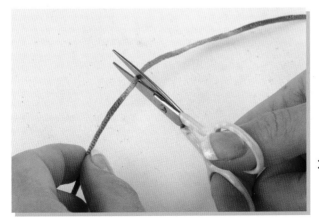

3 Cut your cord to length with embroidery scissors. Measure a further three cords against this first length to give you four equal lengths in total.

BEGINNING YOUR PIECE

The techniques on this page demonstrate how to begin your kumihimo braid. This example shows an eight-braid project, which begins with four strands of cord of equal length.

tip

Tie your cords together using 10cm (4in) surplus cord, ideally in a dark or contrasting colour so it is easy to keep track of as you braid. You will remove the surplus cord at the end of the braiding process.

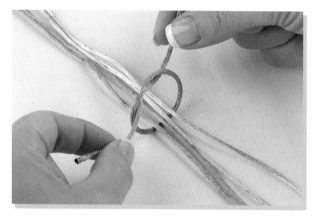

1 After cutting your cord to the required length, lay the four strands together lengthwise. Tie a spare length of cord around the middle of the four lengths – you will remove this surplus length at the end of the braiding process.

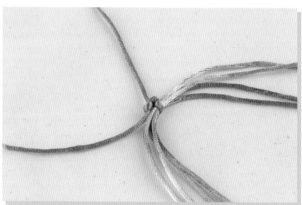

2 Double-knot the surplus cord and pull tight around the four strands.

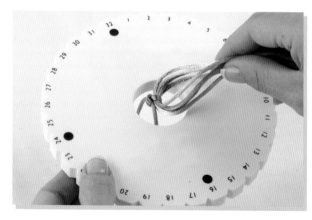

3 Push the knot down through the central hole of the disc, ensuring the tails of the surplus cord are pushed underneath the disc and that they don't get tangled in the lengths of the braid.

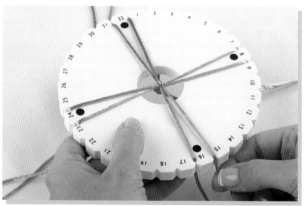

4 Place one length of cord at a time in the foam slot on your disc, depending on the pattern you are creating. The photograph illustrates the formation of a basic eight-braid disc. Take care to keep the knot in the centre of your cords, and don't over-tighten any of the lengths of cord.

5 If you wish to use a weight (see page 11), you can add it now. Clip the weight through the loop made by the four cords.

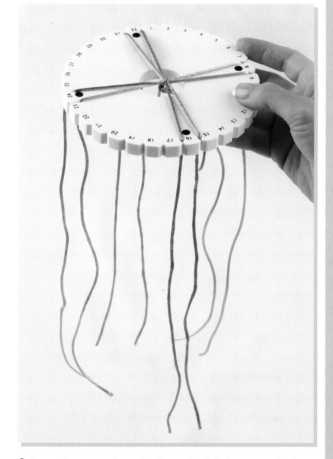

6 Once all your cords are in place, check below your disc to ensure the cords are all of an equal length. If they are not, pull the cords through the disc to even them up. Once you have started braiding, you will not be able to rearrange or adjust the length of your cords so it is important to do it at this stage.

READING THE KUMIHIMO DISC

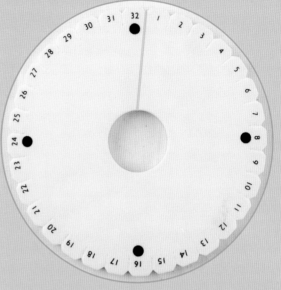

When following the patterns in this book, note that we refer to a number at which to place your cord. This is the slot to the right of the number on the disc. The diagram above shows a cord at number **32**.

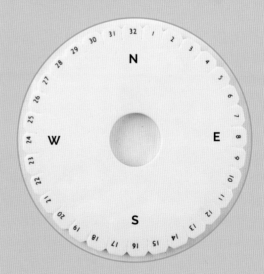

When positioning your cords on a disc, it might help you to think of the kumihimo disc as a compass – imagine number **32** as North (N), **8** as East (E), **16** as South (S) and **24** as West (W).

FINISHING YOUR PIECE

There are various ways in which you can finish your kumihimo braid; while you will typically not be able to see the end of the braid once it is glued into your end cap, the neater you can make your end, the easier it will be to fit it into the cap.

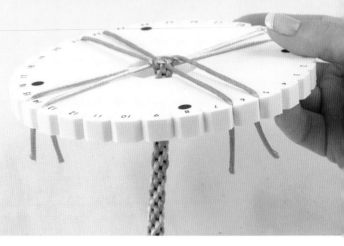

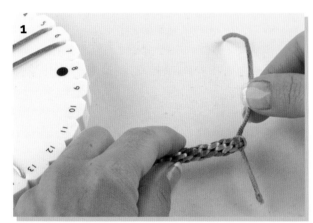

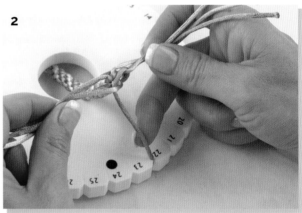

1 Untie and remove the surplus cord from the (bottom) end of the braid.

2 Carefully remove the top of the braid from the disc, removing each cord from its slot one by one.

3 Tie four of the cord ends to the other four cord ends.

4 Tie a length of strong, fine thread around the braid behind the knot; whip the thread around the braid several times to tighten it. Make a further knot to secure the thread in place.

5 Use Hypo cement glue extruded through a thin tip to secure the knot of the thin thread. Allow to dry.

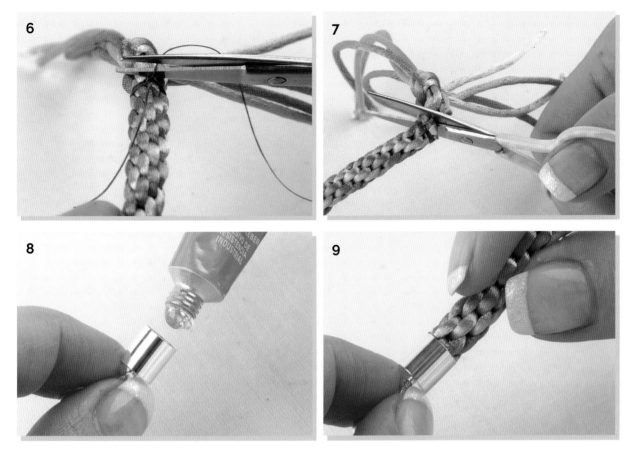

6 When the glue has dried, trim the tails of the thread.

7 Cut off the surplus cord behind the whipping (that is, the knotted strands). Take care not to cut the whipped thread as the braid will unravel.

8 Put glue – E6000 or similar this time – into a small area inside your end cap. Around a third of a cap full is plenty – overfilling the cap with glue will result in it squeezing out of the cap.

9 Twist the end of the braid into the cap to spread the glue around the braid. Allow to dry. Repeat steps 8 and 9 to secure the other end cap to the neat, bottom – or bullet – end of the braid (shown below).

CHOOSING YOUR END CAP

The size of your end cap depends on the size of cord you are using and the pattern you are creating. For a standard eight-braid kumihimo in the materials listed below, choose caps in the following sizes:

- 0.6 macramé cord or S-Lon (used for beaded kumihimo): **5–6mm end cap**
- 1mm satin cord: **6–8mm end cap**
- 2mm satin cord: **8–10mm end cap**

The size of end cap you need for a project may also depend on how neat your finishing is as to whether the cap will fit on the end. You can always bind around the end to use a slightly smaller end cap or add extra glue to pad out the end slightly.

BEADED KUMIHIMO

Once you have mastered the braided kumihimo, why not try a beaded piece? These pages will help you to prepare your cord – ready to add the beads – and introduce a beaded kumihimo pattern.

Follow the instructions on page 13 for guidance on measuring the correct length of cord required for your eight-braid beaded project.

LOADING BEADS ONTO CORD

Preparing your cord before you thread your beads on will make threading the beads much simpler.

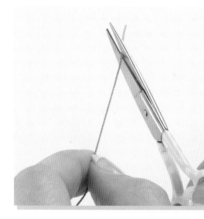

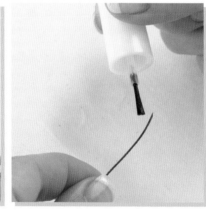

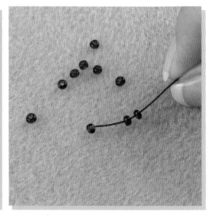

1 Cut the ends of your beading cord at an angle using fine, sharp embroidery scissors.

2 Coat a fine layer of nail polish around 5cm (2in) up the cord. Ensure the cord is coated on all sides but that it does not make the cord too thick to pass through delicate beads. After a few minutes, roll the cord between your fingers to secure the fibres together. Leave to dry until the cord is stiff, like a needle.

3 Pick up the beads from your beading mat with ease!

tip

For an eight-braid beaded kumihimo, roughly fifty beads per cord will create a 17¾cm (7in) bracelet. Another seven beads per cord will add 2½cm (1in) beaded kumihimo if you need additional length.

READING A BEADING PATTERN

There are many ways in which a kumihimo pattern can be shown, and normally kumihimo designers will explain how an individual pattern can be read. The pattern below shows a disc without numbers printed on. The shaded dots around the disc represent the colour and type of bead – or the cord – to be used in that position.

If a beading pattern requires you to add a pattern of beads onto each strand, the dots will represent the colour or type of bead to be added in the sequence required, along with a key to explain the bead(s) needed. I have used some of these throughout the book along with a description of how to add the beads.

The beading pattern below corresponds with the instructions for *Maxine*, the eight-braid cuff (on pages 62–67). The resultant braid is shown below, right.

Above: the disc setup that corresponds with the beading pattern (below left).

○ Seed bead

● Lentil bead

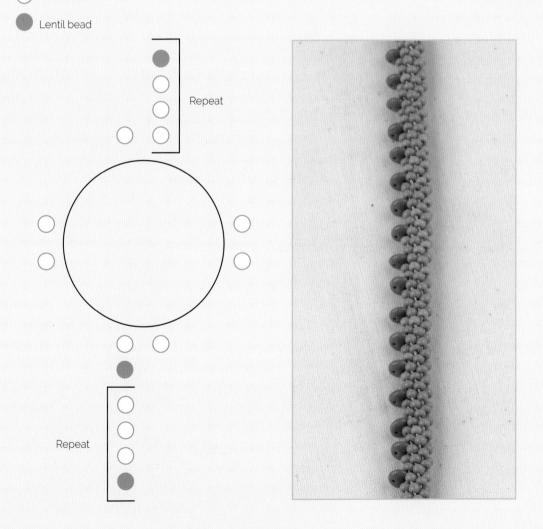

Repeat

Repeat

THE PROJECTS

Audrey Eight-braid bracelet

This eight-braid kumihimo project is a great beginners' braid that will help you understand how the kumihimo process works.

You will need...

- Large kumihimo disc, 15cm (6in) diameter
- 2m (78¾in) 2mm satin cord (pale blue)
- 2m (78¾in) 2mm satin cord (peach)
- 8mm end caps

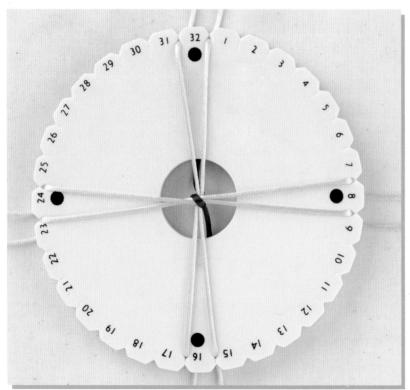

1 Measure and cut your cords following the instructions on page 13; then prepare the cords following the instructions on page 14–15.

Beginning with number **32** at the top of the disc, arrange your cords as follows: place two strands of pale blue cord at numbers **31** and **32**, and two strands at numbers **15** and **16**. Place two strands of peach cord at numbers **7** and **8**, and two strands at numbers **23** and **24**.

tip

Turn the disc ninety degrees anti-clockwise after every two moves.

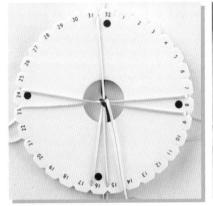

2 Move the pale blue cord at **32** down to **14**.

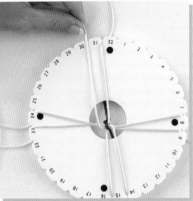

3 Move the pale blue cord at **16** up to **30**.

4 Turn the disc ninety degrees anti-clockwise: this will place number **8** at the top of the disc. Move the peach cord at **8** down to **22**.

5 Move the peach cord at **24** up to **6**.

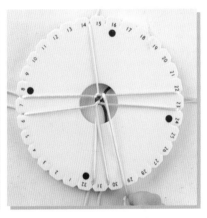

6 Turn the disc anti-clockwise to place number **15** at the top of the disc. Move the pale blue cord at **15** down to **29**.

the point of braiding

As you braid, familiarize yourself with the 'point of braiding' in the centre of the disc (right). You will see a pattern begin to form here as you make a repetition of moves, which will help you to spot if you make a mistake.

7 Move the pale blue cord at **31** up to **13**.

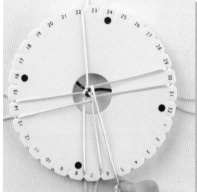

8 Turn the disc anti-clockwise again to place number **23** at the top of the disc. Move the peach cord at **23** down to **5**.

9 Move the peach cord at **7** up to **21**.

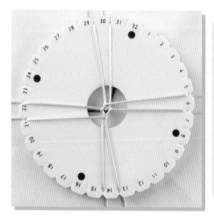

10 Turn the disc anti-clockwise once more to place **30** at the top. The pale blue cords should be at positions **29** and **30** at the top and **13** and **14** at the bottom of the disc; the peach cords should be at positions **5** and **6**, and at **21** and **22**.

tip

At step 11, before you inspect your braiding, move your top-right cord down so that three cords sit at the bottom of the disc before you inspect the braid. This will help you remember where you have left off when you resume braiding.

11 After you have made a few repetitions around the disc, take a look at how your braid is progressing. You should see a neatly striped braid emerging from the centre of the disc.

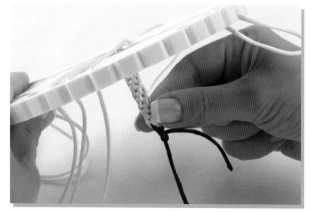

12 Pull the cord gently to get the braid into its natural tension. Repeat the pattern shown in steps 2 to 9, beginning by taking the cord at the top-right of the disc down to the bottom-right, so that the next cord you move will be the pale blue cord at **30**, which moves down to **12**.

TO FINISH YOUR BRACELET

Continue to braid until your bracelet is the desired length, then finish your piece, following the instructions on pages 16–17.

TROUBLESHOOTING

It is normal to make mistakes when you are learning to braid; here are two of the most common mistakes that occur, and how to avoid them.

CROSSING THE CORDS

When you take the bottom-left cord up to the top-left of the disc, move the cord straight upwards. Do not cross the bottom-left cord over the top-right cord as this will cause inconsistency in your braiding.

FORGETTING TO ROTATE YOUR DISC

If you forget to turn your disc anti-clockwise after every two moves, and then move the top-right cord downwards again, the braid will lose its structure. Always rotate your disc to allow for an even braid structure.

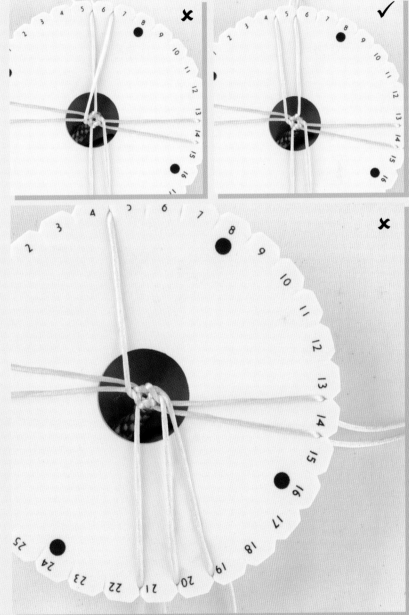

EIGHT-BRAID
BRACELETS

The size and type of the cord
with which you braid will
determine the size of your
finished braid. You can make a
thinner braid by using S-Lon or
0.6mm macramé cord; both of
these braids are ideal for adding
pendants onto your piece.

   The way in which you lay
your cord out on the top of your
disc will change the structure
and the appearance of the
finished braid.

   When you have gained
more confidence, feel free
to experiment with your own
designs. The bracelets shown
on these pages are just a small
selection of the designs that can
be created with simple eight-
braid kumihimo.

LILAC TWIST

- 2m (78¾in) 0.6mm macramé cord in light purple (cord A)
- 2m (78¾in) 0.6mm macramé cord in dark purple (cord B)
- 6mm end cap (silver)

Beginning positions:
Cord A: **24**, **31**, **32** and **7**.
Cord B: **8**, **15**, **16** and **23**.

CANDYFLOSS SWIRL

- 3m (118in) 2mm satin cord in pink (cord A)
- 1m (39¼in) textured yarn (cord B)
- 8mm end cap (rose gold)

Beginning positions:
Cord A: **31**, **32**, **7**, **15**, **16** and **24**.
Cord B: **8** and **23**.

MOCHA STRIPE

- 2m (78¾in) 1mm satin cord in brown (cord A)
- 2m (78¾in) 1mm satin cord in cream (cord B)
- 6mm end cap (gold)

Beginning positions:
Cord A: **31**, **7**, **15** and **23**.
Cord B: **32**, **8**, **16** and **24**.

Donna — Eight-braid beaded bracelet

This eight-braid beaded kumihimo project is a natural progression from the standard eight-braid technique. The sequence of moves that creates this beaded braid is the same sequence as for the basic eight-braid, but with the introduction of beads. I have included some beautiful and interesting variations that you can introduce to your own jewellery pieces.

You will need...

- Large kumihimo disc, 15cm (6in) diameter
- 4m (13ft) 0.5mm S-Lon cord (blue)
- 5g (¼oz) size 8 seed beads (opaque blue)
- 5g (¼oz) size 8 seed beads (transparent blue)
- 5mm end caps

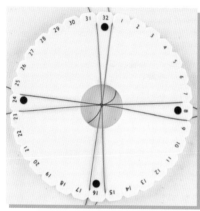

1 Measure your cords (see page 13), lay out the cords as shown on page 15 then prepare the cords for beading, following the instructions on page 18. Set up your disc with the cords in the same positions as shown in step 1, page 22.

2 Following the instructions for basic eight-braid on pages 22–24, braid a 0.5cm (¼in) section without beads. This is the end to which you will glue your end cap. It might help to end the section with your cords in the same positions as in step 1. Then, following the instructions on page 18, prepare your cords, ready to thread on your beads.

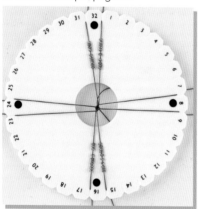

3 Thread fifty transparent blue seed beads on the cords at **31** and **32**, and **15** and **16**.

tip

When threading beads onto your cords, keep ten beads per cord on the top of the disc as you work, and the surplus beads and cord on a bobbin (see opposite page). After you have braided those ten beads, move the next set of ten up onto the top of the disc.

using bobbins

At steps 3 and 4, after you have threaded your beads onto your cords, you may want to wrap your cord and surplus beads onto bobbins to prevent them from tangling.

To use the bobbins, pop them open (into a figure-of-eight shape) and wind your cord and beads around the bobbin. Once you have gathered up most of your cord, pop the bobbin closed.

As you braid, and need more cord and beads, pop open a bobbin, one at a time. Unwind enough cord to enable you to continue with your braiding and take out another ten beads before closing the bobbin again.

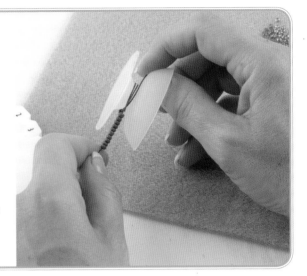

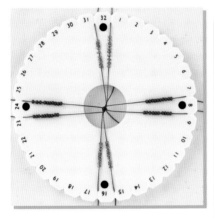

4 Thread fifty opaque blue seed beads on each of the four cords at **7** and **8**, and **23** and **24**.

braiding with beads

As you move each cord, push one bead down and rest it on the outside of the cord it is crossing. The photograph here illustrates the correct position of a bead passed from top-right (**32**) to bottom-right (**14**) over position **7**.

5 Begin to braid, following the same sequence as for basic eight-braid. The first moves you make will be to move the cord at **32** down to **14** – popping a bead under the cord before you move it down – then move the cord at **16** up to **30**, and so on.

6 Repeat this on the cord you are taking up, again popping a bead down under the cord you are crossing before you put the cord in place.

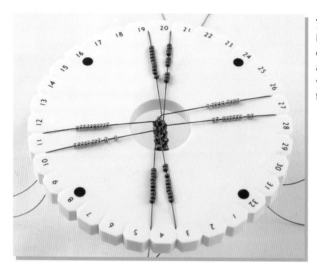

7 Rotate the disc anti-clockwise and repeat steps 5 and 6 Remember to add a bead as you take each cord over and ensure none of the other beads slides into the centre as you are working. When you have used the ten beads per cord that you have on your disc, undo your bobbins (if you are using them) and slide ten more beads up onto each cord.

FINISHING OFF

1 Remove your cord from the disc. Tie off any loose ends

2 Whip a length of thread around the ends (see page 16).

3 Cut off the ends beyond the whipped cord.

4 Finally, attach the end caps following the instructions on page 17.

The completed eight-braid beaded bracelet.

EIGHT-BRAID BEADED KUMIHIMO VARIATIONS

Once you have mastered the basics of eight-braid beaded kumihimo, you can experiment with beads of all sizes, shapes and colours to create unlimited design variations. Have fun co-ordinating your beaded kumihimo pieces to your wardrobe.

   The instructions for creating the three variation bracelets seen here are on the following pages.

TWO-SIZED BEADED DESIGN

To create this twist, you will need to vary the size of beads that you use. Some beads work better with others – use two sets of beads with a size difference of two or three to create the perfect twist. For this example, I have used size 6 beads with size 8 beads.

- 4m (13ft) 0.5mm S-Lon cord (gold)
- 14g (½oz) size 6 seed beads (multicoloured)
- 10g (¼oz) size 8 seed beads (gold)
- 5mm end caps

Set up the cords following the instructions for beaded kumihimo on page 28. Thread thirty-five size 6 beads onto cords **31** and **32**, **15** and **16**. Thread thirty-five size 8 beads onto cords **7** and **8**, **23** and **24**.

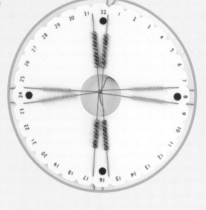

SILVER DOTTY DESIGN

This bracelet has a sparkly highlight with a crystal dot feature around the braid.

- 4m (13ft) 0.5mm S-Lon cord (bronze)
- 50 4mm bicone crystals
- 350 4mm glass pearls
- 5mm end caps

Set up the cord as per the beaded kumihimo instructions on page 28 and thread around fifty 4mm pearls onto each of the cords at **15**, **23** and **24**, **31**, **7** and **8**.
   Follow the beading pattern on the right to thread crystals and pearls onto cords **32** and **16** until you have fifty beads on each cord altogether. Then begin to braid following the instructions on page 29.

THE BEADING PATTERN

○ Crystal

○ Pearl

Repeat

Repeat

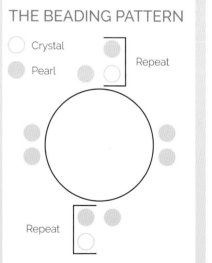

MAGATAMA BEADED KUMIHIMO

Magatama beads create a tactile bracelet due to the angled shape of the beads and the off-centre position of the hole in the bead.

- 4m (13ft) 0.5mm S-Lon cord (pale lilac)
- 120 long magatama beads (matt amethyst)
- 120 long magatama beads (amethyst)
- 5mm end caps

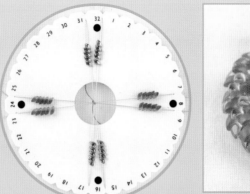

Set up your cords as per the beaded kumihimo instructions on page 28. Position your cords at numbers **31** and **32**, **7** and **8**, **15** and **16**, and **23** and **24**. Thread thirty magatama beads in amethyst onto **31** and **32**, and **15** and **16**. Thread thirty magatama beads in matt amethyst on **7** and **8**, **23** and **24**.

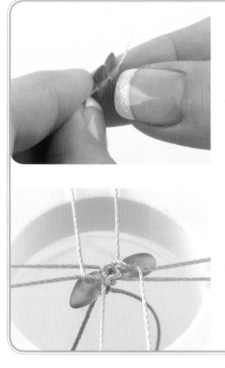

working with magatama beads

When you are threading on the magatama beads, the direction in which you thread the beads is important. As you add the beads to the cord at steps 1 and 2, make sure they all face in the same direction as shown in the photograph on the left.

When you slide the magatama beads in place and move the cords over, make sure you position the short end of the bead under the cord so that the long end faces outwards and creates the spiky effect you see in the finished piece above.

Loraine 'Inside-out' bracelet

This inside-out beaded kumihimo is a simple variation on the eight-braided beaded design – the main difference is that the beads sit on the inside of the cord, and the cord is visible on the outside. The placement of beads is trickier but worth the effort!

You will need...

- Large kumihimo disc, 15cm (6in) diameter
- 6m (19¾ft) 0.5mm S-Lon cord (red)
- 14g (½oz) size 8 seed beads (red)
- 16mm (¾in)-diameter button with four holes
- Sewing needle
- Beading thread for whipping

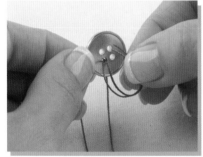

NOTE

Within this project you will also learn to make a button and loop fastening, which is a comfortable alternative to a metal fastening or end cap. Bear in mind that the loop fastening will add another 2½cm (1in) length to this bracelet, which is otherwise 17¾ (7in) long.

1 Cut four 1.5m (5ft) lengths of cord. Place two strands together and thread up through one hole in the button and down through the hole diagonally opposite.

2 Take the other two strands and thread them up and back down through the other pair of holes to form a cross. Pull all the cords through so the button is in the middle of the cord lengths.

3 Place the button, face down, in the centre of your disc, ready for the cords to be laid out in step 4.

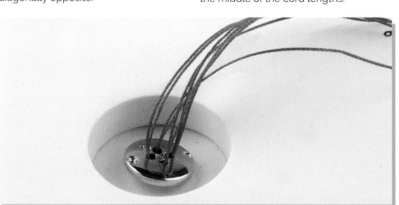

tip

With this braid, each bead is not secured in place until you braid two more cords on top of it – you will need to take care that the bead does not pop off the top of the braid until it is secured by a cord.

4 Prepare your cords for beading (following the instructions on page 18) then lay out your cords at positions **31** and **32**, **7** and **8**, **15** and **16**, and **23** and **24**. Braid 0.5cm (¼in) cord directly above the button without any beads on. Thread forty size 8 beads onto each of your cords.

5 You are now ready to start integrating the beads. As you move a cord over in sequence, rest one bead on top of the centre of the cords it is crossing, before placing the cord into its new slot. Continue braiding and adding your beads in this way until your braid is the desired length.

MAKING THE LOOP FASTENING

1 Braid the end of your cord in standard eight-braid (see pages 22–24) to a length of 60mm (2¼in). Add a drop of Hypo cement glue to the centre of the braid to seal it. Then remove the braid from the disc.

2 Thread a sewing needle with one of the loose ends of the braid, and feed the thread back through the braid at the top of the beaded cord.

3 Fold the braided loop over and thread the needle all the way through the braid.

4 Repeat steps 2–3 to thread the other loose ends to the braid, until you have a complete loop. Add a drop of Hypo cement glue to the threads as they come through the braid.

5 With sharp scissors, cut off all but one of the loose threads.

6 Cut a surplus piece of cord to a length of 10cm (4in). Fold the surplus cord into a loop and place it on top of the looped braid.

7 Bind the long piece of cord from the braid around the base of the braided loop and the base of the surplus cord loop. Wrap the long cord around the two loops about ten times but make sure the braided loop is still loose enough to slip comfortably over the button fastening.

8 Thread the loose cord up through the loop made with the surplus cord from behind.

9 Hold both ends of the surplus cord loop and pull it down through the binding from step 7.

10 Use the surplus cord to pull the loose cord through the binding as well. Then release the surplus loop and thread the loose cord back through the braid to secure it.

11 Finally, trim off any excess ends and add a final drop of glue to secure the binding.

'INSIDE-OUT' BRACELETS

The button and loop fastening is just one option for how you can embellish an 'inside-out' bracelet. You can make your button and loop fastening more decorative by adding a tassel from the button, as shown below, on the blue bracelet.

Margaret
Infinity knot necklace

This eight-braid project teaches you to create a blended, beaded kumihimo necklace. This technique is combined with the creation of an infinity knot, which can symbolize eternity and everlasting love. This is a stunning project that will help you develop – and advance – your kumihimo skills.

This necklace consists of two sections: bottom and top. We begin by creating the bottom section.

You will need...

- Large kumihimo disc, 15cm (6in) diameter
- 22m (72ft) 0.5mm S-Lon cord (cream)
- 25g (1oz) size 8 seed beads (gold)
- 30g (1oz) size 8 seed beads (bronze)
- Six large-holed beads
- 5mm end caps

BOTTOM SECTION

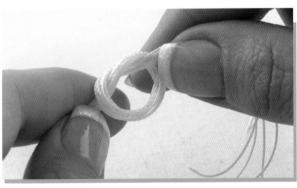

1 Cut eight 1.25m (4ft) lengths of cord – the cord length will result in a bottom section that is 40¾cm (16in) long. Place all eight strands together and tie a knot 10cm (4in) from the end.

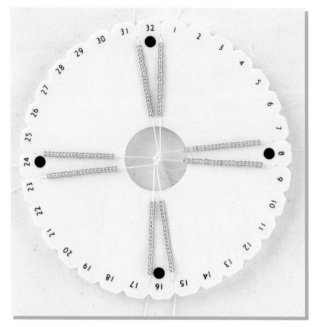

tip

At step 2, you will find it useful to tie a knot in each strand and wind the excess cord and beads round bobbins (see page 29) to stop the cords and the beads tangling.

2 Prepare your cords for beaded kumihimo and lay them out on the disc at positions **31** and **32**, **7** and **8**, **15** and **16**, and **23** and **24**. Braid 0.5cm (¼in) cord without beads – this will become part of the tassel, which you will complete on page 41. Thread twenty size 8 gold beads onto each strand.

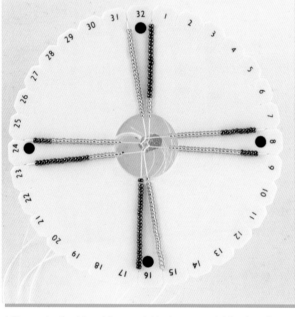

3 Following the instructions for basic eight-braid beading on pages 28–30, begin to braid the gold beads until you have used up all twenty on each strand.

4 To create the blend from gold to bronze, add the beads to the strands in the following quantities:

- twenty-five gold beads onto **31** and **15**
- five gold beads and twenty bronze beads onto **32**
- twenty gold and five bronze beads onto **8** and **24**
- ten gold and fifteen bronze beads onto **23**
- twenty-five bronze onto **16**
- fifteen gold and ten bronze onto **7**.

Braid until you have used up all of these beads.

The gold to bronze blend in progress.

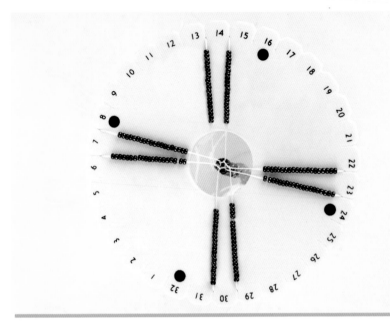

The braid in progress at step 5.

5 Thread another twenty bronze seed beads to each of your eight strands, and braid again.

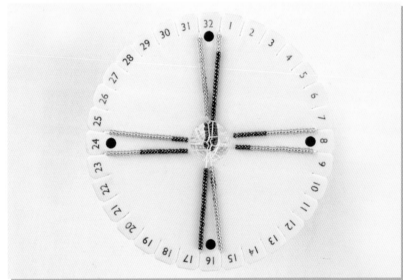

The braid in progress at step 6.

6 To create the reverse blend from bronze to gold, add the beads to the strands in the following quantities:

- twenty-five gold beads onto **31** and **15**
- twenty bronze and five gold beads onto **32**
- five bronze and twenty gold beads onto **8** and **24**
- fifteen bronze and ten gold beads onto **23**
- twenty-five bronze beads onto **16**
- ten bronze and fifteen gold beads onto **7.**

Braid until you have used up all of these beads, then add twenty more gold beads onto each strand. Finish off the bottom section by braiding 0.5cm (¼in) cord without beads and remove the piece from the disc.

MAKING THE TASSELS

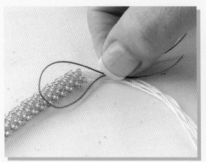

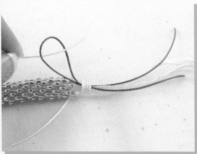

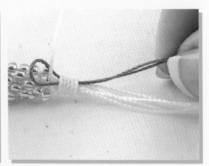

1 Cut a 10cm (4in) length of surplus cord or beading thread. Create a loop with the surplus and place it onto the end of the braid. Leave the tails accessible.

2 Pick up one long strand of loose cord. Starting from the base of the beaded braid, bind up the loop of surplus thread approximately five times. Then thread the loose cord up through the surplus loop.

3 Pull both ends of the surplus loop down through the binding. Then trim off the surplus thread and add a dab of glue to the binding to secure it.

4 Thread three large-holed gold beads onto the end of the braid, over the binding.

5 Tie a knot underneath the three beads and add a drop of glue to secure them.

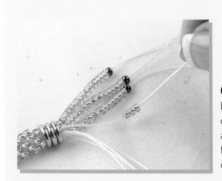

6 Thread around sixteen to twenty gold beads, and one bronze bead, onto each of the tassels. Tie a knot in the end and add a drop of glue to secure. Repeat these steps to create the tassel at the other end of your braid.

TOP SECTION

The process for making the top section of the necklace is very similar to the process for making the bottom section (see pages 38–40). The only differences are that you will be creating a longer braid – 61cm (24in) when complete – and attaching end caps and fasteners.

1 To make the top section of the necklace, cut four 3m (9ft) lengths of cord. Place all four strands together and tie them in the centre with a length of surplus cord.

2 Prepare your cords for beaded kumihimo and lay them out on the disc at positions **31** and **32**, **7** and **8**, **15** and **16**, and **23** and **24**. Braid 0.5cm (¼in) cord without beads – this will glue into an end cap (see page 17).

3 Thread fifty bronze beads onto each strand.

4 You will then need to create the blend from bronze to gold; add the beads to the strands in the following quantities:
- twenty-five bronze beads onto **31** and **15**
- five bronze and twenty gold beads onto **32**
- twenty bronze and five gold beads onto **8** and **24**
- ten bronze and fifteen gold beads onto **23**
- twenty-five gold beads onto **16**
- fifteen bronze and ten gold beads onto **7**.

NOTE

The full length of the completed, linked necklace is 96½cm (38in).

5 Continue to add twenty gold beads to each strand.

6 To create the reverse blend from gold to bronze, add the beads to the strands in the following quantities:
- twenty-five bronze beads onto **31** and **15**
- twenty gold and five bronze beads onto **32**
- five gold and twenty bronze beads onto **8** and **24**
- fifteen gold and ten bronze beads onto **23**
- twenty-five gold beads onto **16**
- ten gold and fifteen bronze beads onto **7**.

7 Continue to add fifty bronze beads onto each strand.

8 Finish this project with 0.5cm (¼in) braided cord and attach your end cap to this part of the necklace.

CREATING THE INFINITY KNOT

1 Fold your two braids in half (in the middle of each blended section).

2 Place the shorter length (the bottom half) over the longer length (the top half) so that the loops 'top and tail'. Slide the two ends of the bottom half under the loop of the top half.

3 Pull the tail ends of the bottom half towards you to tighten the knot.

MARGARET

The completed infinity knot necklace is a stunning piece of jewellery that would be a statement piece that can be worn with any outfit.

INFINITY KNOT VARIATIONS

Create an infinity knot bracelet using beads in two different colours – such as the two shown here. The blend technique can be simplified in order to make a single bracelet, or the necklace shown above.

THE BRACELET

To create the bracelet, cut eight 1m (3ft) lengths of cord. Follow the eight-braid beaded instructions to create two braids in different colours – here, I have used size 8 peach seed beads and size 8 silver-lined peach seed beads. Bring both ends of the braid together and attach an end cap onto both ends to secure.

Follow the instructions on page 42 to create the infinity knot.

THE NECKLACE

You can use the blending methods shown on pages 39, 40 and 42 to create a blend between any two colours. This necklace starts with one colour of bead and blends to another in the middle and then continues in the second colour.

The blend uses twenty-five beads and around 10cm (4in) to change from one bead colour to another.

Jenny Four-colour stripe bracelet

This four-colour bracelet is made by threading beads accurately onto specific strands of cord to determine the finished pattern.

You will need...

- Large kumihimo disc, 15cm (6in) diameter
- 4m (13ft) 0.5mm S-Lon cord (grey)
- 2.5g size 8 seed beads (silver)
- 2.5g size 8 seed beads (silver-lined teal)
- 2.5g size 8 seed beads (matt purple)
- 2.5g size 8 seed beads (matt teal)
- 5mm end caps

THE BEADING PATTERN

- Purple
- Silver
- Matt teal
- Silver-lined teal

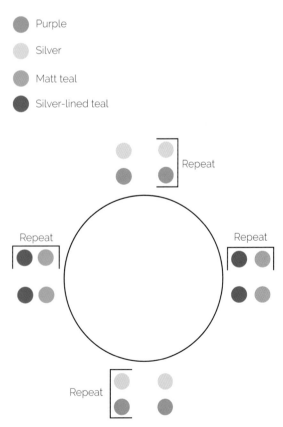

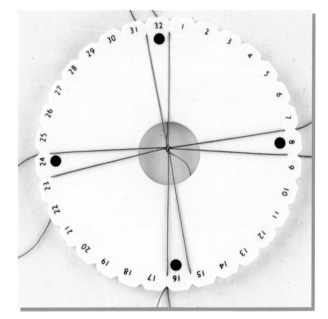

1 Measure and cut your cords into four 1m (39¼in) lengths then lay out the cords on your disc at positions **31** and **32**, **7** and **8**, **15** and **16**, and **23** and **24**. Prepare the cords for beading.

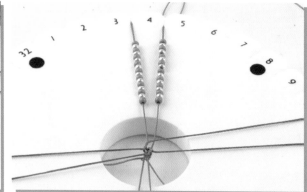

2 Braid 0.5cm (¼in) of cord without beads – this is the end you will glue into the end cap. Prepare your disc so that the next cord you are due to bring down is at the top-right of the disc.

3 Starting with a purple bead, then a silver bead, thread alternate purple and silver beads onto the threads at the top of the disc (here, at positions **3** and **4**) until you have fifty beads on each strand.

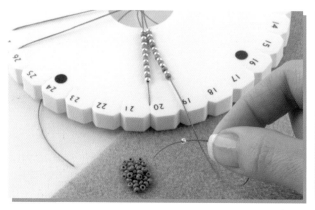

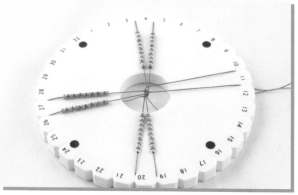

4 Starting with a silver bead, then a purple bead, thread alternate silver and purple beads onto the threads at the bottom of your disc (here, at positions **19** and **20**) until you have fifty beads on each strand.

5 Starting with a matt teal bead, then a silver-lined teal bead, thread alternate matt teal and silver-lined teal beads onto the cords on the left of your disc (here, positions **26** and **27**).

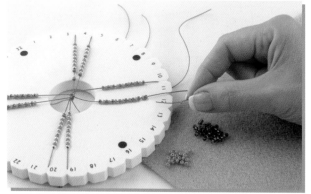

6 Starting with a silver-lined teal bead, then a matt teal bead, thread alternate silver-lined teal and matt teal beads onto the cords on the right of your disc (here, positions **10** and **11**).

Below, your kumihimo disc, ready for braiding.

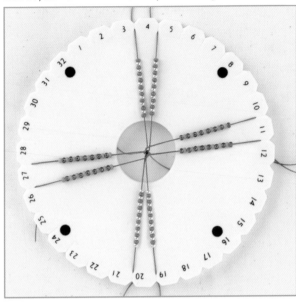

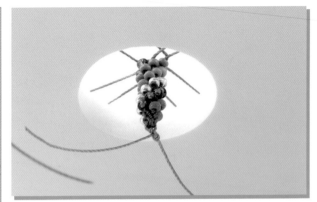

7 Start to braid from the top-right cord – in the photograph on the left, this is cord **4**. Bring in one bead on each move, following the instructions for eight-braid beaded kumihimo on pages 28–30. Make sure that the bead goes under the cord in the centre of the disc (see page 29). Lift up your disc after a few moves to check that your four-stripe beaded cord is looking neat and no beads are out of place.

Continue braiding until your bracelet is the desired length, then follow the instructions on pages 16–17 to remove the braid from the disc and attach an end cap.

tip

You must be accurate when adding your beads for this project. Ensure that you add – and braid in – a bead every time you move a cord over the disc, otherwise your pattern will not work correctly. Your beads must go under the cord.

The finished four-stripe bracelet.
You will notice that the pattern in which you thread on your beads for this piece creates four separate stripes. This pattern will expand your beaded design variations even further.

THE CRYSTAL AND PEARL VARIATION

To create this variation I have used 4mm crystals and pearls, and size 8 seed beads. The seed beads are added to the two cords at the right and the left of the disc, and the crystals and pearls alternated on the two cords at the top and the bottom of the disc. This arrangement results in the two stripes of seed beads and alternating stripes of pearls and crystals shown below.

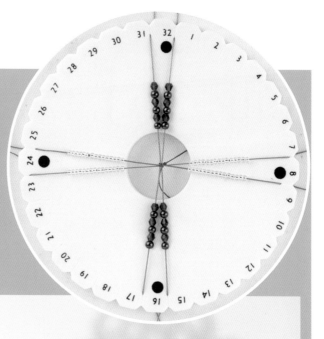

Julie Flower motif bracelet

This pretty eight-braid bracelet, with floral pattern, is made by threading the beads onto specific strands to create the daisy motif. You can easily change the types of bead you use to vary your own finished pieces.

You will need...

- Large kumihimo disc, 15cm (6in) diameter
- 4m (13ft) 0.5mm S-Lon cord (lilac)
- 4g (⅛oz) size 8 seed beads (white)
- 1g (¹/₃₂oz) size 8 seed beads (gold or yellow)
- 6g (¼oz) size 8 seed beads (purple)
- 5mm end caps

1 Measure and cut your cords into four 1m (39¼in) lengths, then lay them out on your disc at positions **31** and **32**, **7** and **8**, **15** and **16**, and **23** and **24**. Prepare the cords for beading, then braid 0.5cm (¼in) without beads – this is the end that you will glue into your end cap. Place the disc so that the next cord you are due to bring down is at the top-right of the disc. This is an important part of the flowers forming correctly when you braid.

Thread fifty white beads onto cords **31** and **32** – these beads will form part of the flower petals.

On cord **7**, beginning with gold, thread alternating gold and purple seed beads – the gold beads will form the flower centres. Thread fifty beads altogether onto this cord.

On cord **8**, beginning with a white bead, thread alternating white and purple seed beads until you have fifty beads altogether on the cord. Do the same on cord **24**, but start with a purple bead and alternate with white until there are fifty beads altogether on the cord.

Thread fifty purple seed beads each onto cords **15**, **16** and **23**.

tip

You will find it useful to tie a knot in each strand and wind the excess cord and beads around bobbins (see page 29) to stop the cords and the beads tangling.

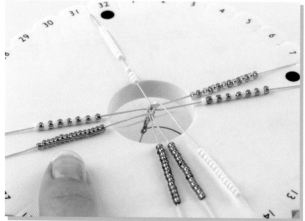

2 Start to braid from the top-right cord (**32**) and bring over one bead per move, following the instructions for eight-braid beaded kumihimo on pages 28–30.

3 After just one full repetition around the disc, your braid will begin to come through the bottom of the disc and the flower pattern will start to form. Continue until your braid is the desired length. If you need to add more beads, undo your knots and add more as required. Remember to do this when you still have at least three beads left on each strand to enable you to see which pattern of beads is on each strand.

INCLUDING A LEAF COMPONENT

To include a leaf component within the flower motif, I have used a miyuki drop bead, but you can use a magatama or simply a seed bead. Once you have arranged your cords on the disc and braided 0.5cm (¼in) cord without beads, thread your leaf bead onto the bottom-left cord – in the photograph on the right, this is cord **16**. Then alternate threading green leaf beads and beads for the colour of the main braid (here, purple), until you have fifty beads threaded on the cord.

tip

You must be accurate with your braiding and add a bead every time you move over a cord; otherwise your pattern will become mixed up and the flower motif will not appear.

FLOWER MOTIF BRACELETS

To create a braid using magatama beads to form the flowers, the sequence of adding the beads onto the cord is the same as for the main flower motif bracelet itself. The result, however, with these uniquely shaped magatama beads, is a tactile, contemporary piece of jewellery that will doubtless attract a lot of attention.

MAGATAMA FLOWER MOTIF BRACELET

The crucial consideration for creating the magatama variation is the direction in which the individual magatama beads are added onto the cord. It is not essential to position each bead specifically, but it will help you to sit the petals more openly on the braid.

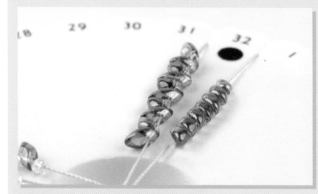

The magatamas on cord **31** are threaded long end up, long end down, alternately. On cords **32** and **8**, the magatama beads are all threaded with the long end down.

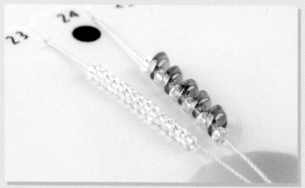

On cord **24**, the magatama bead is threaded on first, long end pointing up, followed by a small translucent seed bead.

Follow the eight-braid beaded instructions to braid this piece. You will need to ensure the magatama beads do not get caught within the braid. If they do get caught, however, this is easy to spot and correct, even if you are further along your braid.

Jade Beaded popper charm bracelet

This beaded kumihimo bracelet has an interchangeable popper charm so you can easily and simply change the finished look of your bracelet. This project also introduces the technique of beading from a centrepiece outwards, towards an end fastening.

The initial arrangement of beads for this project creates a braid that has a double stripe running through it.

You will need...

- Small kumihimo disc, 11cm (4¼in) diameter
- 5.6m (18¼ft) 0.5mm S-Lon cord (white or cream)
- Double-ended popper finding
- Popper charm of your choice
- Two large-holed spacer beads
- 4g (⅛oz) size 8 seed beads (gold)
- 10g (¼oz) size 6 pearl seed beads (cream)
- 5mm end caps

1 Cut four pieces of cord each to 70cm (27½in) lengths. Place the four strands together and thread them through one side of your popper finding.

2 Fold the lengths in half again. Thread a large-holed spacer bead over all eight strands and over the loop of the popper finding.

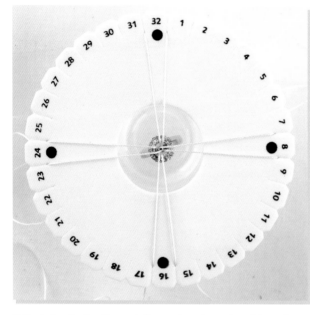

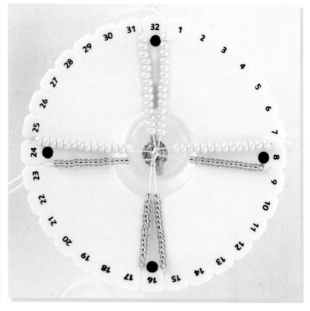

3 Push the finding through the centre of your kumihimo disc as you would the knot on a standard eight-braid. Then lay the cords out as for an eight-braid kumihimo – at positions **31** and **32**, **7** and **8**, **15** and **16**, and **23** and **24**. Prepare your cords for beading then braid 0.5cm (¼in) cord without beads, to feed into the large-holed spacer.

4 Prepare your disc so that the next cord you are due to bring down is at the top-right of the disc (**32**). Thread fifteen size 6 cream beads apiece on cords **24**, **31**, **32** and **7**, then thread fifteen size 8 gold seed beads apiece on cords **8**, **15**, **16** and **23**.

5 Begin to braid the cord, following the instructions for beaded kumihimo on pages 28–30. Take care when you integrate the first few beads to ensure that they sit directly above the large-holed spacer, and that each bead sits underneath the cords in the centre of the disc.

6 When your beaded braid reaches your desired length, finish it off by braiding another 0.5cm (¼in) cord without beads.

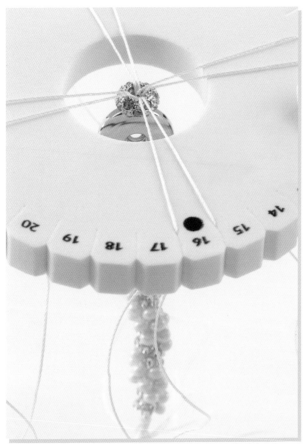

7 Remove your braid from the disc. Then, follow steps 1 to 6 to create the other half of your bracelet in exactly the same way. Following the instructions on page 17, attach an end cap to each braided end of the bracelet.

8 Finally, pop your chosen detachable centrepiece (the popper charm) onto the bracelet – attach it directly to the popper fastening.

The finished bracelet.

BEADED POPPER
CHARM BRACELETS

Pinch beads are three-sided beads that sit beautifully on a kumihimo project. After you have set up your cord and threaded on a large-holed bead, thread eight pinch beads onto each strand of cord. You will need to ensure that each pinch bead is positioned correctly on the cord as they are longer than seed beads, but the results are worth the attention and effort.

Gaynor Crystal kumihimo necklace

This elegant necklace introduces a variety of different beads
to create a graduated braid and a feature centrepiece.

You will need...

- Large kumihimo disc, 15cm (6in) diameter
- 8m (26¼ft) 0.5mm S-Lon cord (grey)
- 12g (½oz) size 8 seed beads (silver-lined transparent)
- 8g (¼oz) size 6 seed beads (silver)
- Sixty 4mm glass pearls (silver)
- Forty 4 x 6mm crystal rondelles (half coated silver)
- Twenty 6 x 8mm crystal rondelles (half coated silver)
- 5mm end caps

From left to right: 8mm crystal rondelle, 6mm crystal rondelle, 4mm glass pearl, size 6 seed bead; size 8 seed bead.

NOTE

The cord measurements given will result in a necklace that is 43¼cm (17in) long.

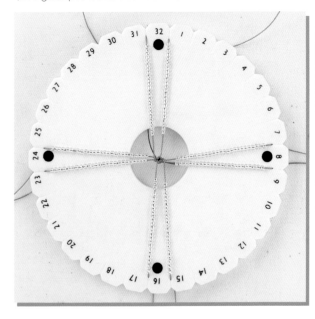

tip

To keep the longer strands of crystals and beads from
tangling, tie a knot in the end of each cord and wrap
each cord around a bobbin.

1 Cut four pieces of cord to a length of 2m (6½ft) each, and tie
in the centre with 10cm (4in) surplus cord. Lay out your cords
at positions **31** and **32**, **7** and **8**, **15** and **16**, and **23** and **24**.
Prepare the cord for beading, then braid 0.5cm (¼in) of cord
without beads, to glue into the end cap at step 5.

- Thread twenty-five size 8 seed beads onto all eight cords.
- Thread a further sixty-five size 8 seed beads onto the
  cords at **31** and **15** so each strand will have a total of ninety
  beads on it.

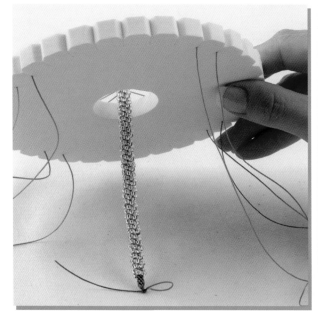

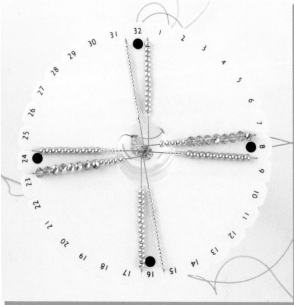

2 Braid the beaded cords following the instructions for basic eight-braid beading on pages 28–30 until you run out of beads on the disc.

3 Onto cords **32** and **16,** thread forty size 6 beads and a further twenty-five size 8 beads.

Onto cords **7** and **23**, thread five size 6 beads; ten 4 x 6mm crystal rondelles; ten 6 x 8mm crystal rondelles; another ten 4 x 6mm crystal rondelles; another five size 6 beads; and a further twenty-five size 8 beads.

Onto cords **8** and **24**, thread five size 8 beads; thirty 4mm pearls; and finally thirty size 8 beads. Tie a knot in each end of your cord and wrap round your bobbins.

4 Start to braid the cords again, following the instructions for beaded kumihimo on pages 28–30.

tip

As the braid comes through, gently pull it down to its natural tension and squeeze the beads to help the crystals sit in place without being too tightly bound together.

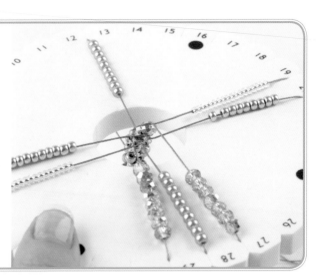

tip

As you braid the different-sized beads and move from the smaller beads to the larger beads, ensure the beads sit correctly on the braid. In particular, ensure that the largest crystals are tucked correctly under the cord as it is passed over the centre of the disc, to minimize gaps on the cord.

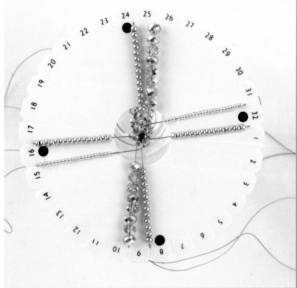

5 Continue braiding until your necklace has reached its desired length, or until you run out of beads. Braid 0.5cm (¼in) without beads to finish. Remove the piece from the disc and attach the end cap and fastener, following the instructions on pages 16–17.

The near-complete necklace.

GAYNOR

The completed crystal kumihimo necklace, which will undoubtedly add sparkle and elegance to a Little Black Dress

Maxine Eight-braid cuff

This feature cuff is created from two beaded kumihimo braids. The lentil beads are carefully placed between the two braids to enable a simple beadweaving feature in the centre.

You will need...

- Large kumihimo disc, 15cm (6in) diameter
- 8m (26¼ft) 0.5mm S-Lon cord (light blue)
- 20g (¾oz) size 8 seed beads (opaque teal)
- Fifty 6mm lentil beads (Parisian turquoise)
- Twenty-five 6mm glass pearls (teal)
- Fifty-four 3 x 4mm crystal rondelles
- Magnetic wide end caps
- Beading needle
- 2m (6½ft) beading thread

NOTE

The cord measurements and bead quantities I have listed here will create a cuff that is approximately 20¼cm (8in) long.

THE BEADING PATTERN

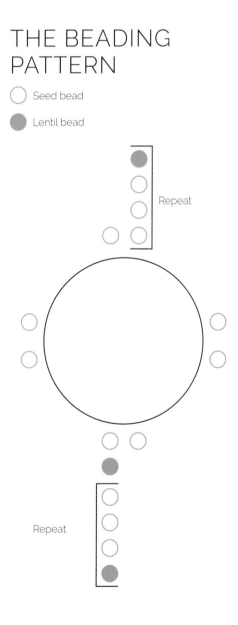

○ Seed bead

● Lentil bead

Repeat

Repeat

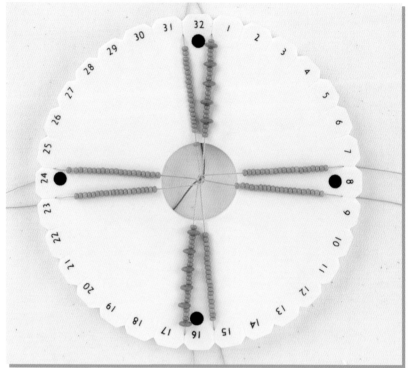

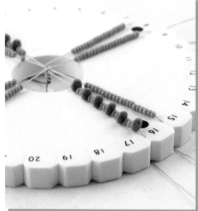

1 Cut four 1m (39¼in) lengths of cord and tie in the centre with 10cm (4in) surplus cord. Lay out the cords at positions **31** and **32**, **15** and **16**, **7** and **8**, and **23** and **24**. Prepare your cords for beading, then braid 0.5cm (¼in) without beads to glue into your end cap. Try to ensure that your cords end up in the same starting positions. Make sure that the next move you make will be to move the top-right cord (here, **32**) down to the bottom-right of the disc (**14**). This is important in ensuring that the lentil beads will sit correctly.

Following the beading pattern on the opposite page, and the photograph above, thread fifty-one size 8 seed beads onto strands **31**, **7**, **8**, **15**, **23** and **24**.

Thread three size 8 beads and one lentil bead onto cord **32**. Repeat until you have fifty-one beads altogether on cord **32** – keep about twenty beads on the top of the disc at one time, with the remaining beads wrapped around a bobbin.

2 On cord **16,** thread on one seed bead and one lentil bead, followed by three seed beads and one lentil bead. Repeat the pattern of threading three seed beads then one lentil bead until you have fifty-one beads altogether on cord **16**. Tie a knot in the end of each cord and wrap the excess around a bobbin.

3 Start to braid, following the instructions for eight-braid beaded kumihimo on pages 28–30. The way in which you have threaded the beads at steps 1 and 2 will ensure that the lentil beads will sit on one side of the braid.

Make sure that the beads sit under the cords they cross in the middle of the disc.

Once you have braided all of the beads on the disc, braid 0.5cm (¼in) cord without beads, then remove the braid from the disc.

tip

The braid can sometimes twist slightly underneath the disc – if this happens, twist it back in the opposite direction.

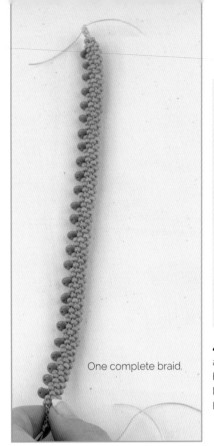

One complete braid.

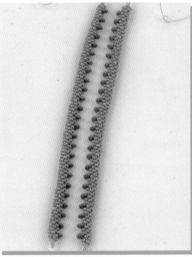

4 Repeat steps 1–3 on page 63 to create a second, identical braid. Lay the two braids together so that the lentil beads line up on the inside edges of the braids, like tramlines.

5 Thread 2m (6½ft) of beading thread onto your needle. Thread down through the lentil bead at the bottom of the left-hand braid, leaving a tail of about 10cm (4in) of thread.

6 Holding on to your tail of thread, pick up a crystal, then a pearl, then another crystal on your needle. Pass the needle back up through the first (bottom) lentil bead on the right-hand braid.

7 Pick up another crystal, pearl and crystal. Tie off the working thread with the tail you have been holding to create a circle of beads on the braid. Cut off the tail, then secure the knot on the braid with a drop of glue.

8 Take the needle back down through the bottom-left lentil bead...

9 ...back through the bottom row containing the crystal, pearl and crystal...

10 ...up through the bottom-right lentil bead, and left again, back through the crystal and pearl in the second row.

11 Pick up a new crystal on the needle. Pass the needle and thread up through the next lentil on the left.

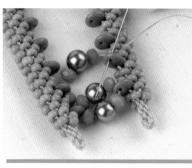

12 Pick up another crystal, pearl and crystal on the needle. Take the needle down through the next lentil bead on the right.

13 Pick up another crystal on the needle. Pass left through the pearl and the top crystal in the middle row.

14 Pass the needle back up through the left lentil bead.

15 Continue right through the top crystal and pearl towards the right of the cuff.

16 Pick up another crystal and pass up through the next lentil bead on the right.

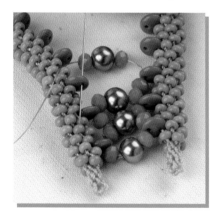

17 Thread on a crystal, pearl and crystal, and take the needle down through the next lentil bead on the left. Pick up another crystal.

18 Pass the needle and thread right back through the pearl and crystal, and up through the lentil bead on the right of the cuff.

19 Continue to thread through the next crystal and pearl, back towards the left of the cuff.

20 Repeat steps 11 to 19 all the way up the cuff until you reach the braided ends.

21 To finish the cuff, add a crystal, a pearl and a crystal, take the needle down through the next lentil bead then thread on the last crystal.

22 Pass the needle back through the final circle of beads and knot the thread with a lark's head knot. Add a drop of glue to secure the knot then trim off the ends of the thread.

23 Dab glue into a wide end cap at both ends then place onto the one end of the double braid so that the glue secures both sides of the braid. Repeat for the opposite end of your cuff to complete, and lay the cuff out flat to dry.

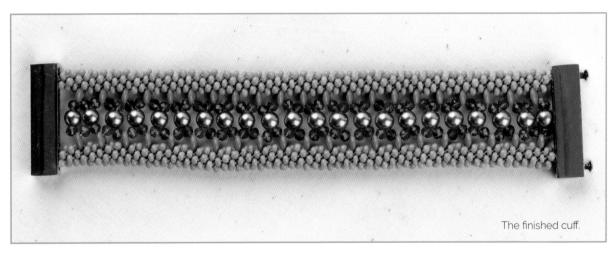

The finished cuff.

ROSE-GOLD AND BRONZE CUFF VARIATION (OPPOSITE)

The design of this cuff is identical to the teal cuff, created with rose-gold seed and lentil beads, bronze pearls and creamy crystals for a glorious autumnal colour variation.

Once you have mastered the method of threading together the two halves of the cuff, you can create this piece in your own varied and vivid colour schemes.

Jodie Simple seven-braid bracelet

This kumihimo project uses seven strands of cord – and a new repetition of moves – to create a different braid structure.

Once you are confident with the method of working with seven cords, you can introduce beads to your own pieces, which will give you many more design possibilities.

You will need...

- Large kumihimo disc, 15cm (6in) diameter
- Seven 60cm (23½in) strands of 1mm satin cord (in assorted colours)
- 8mm end caps

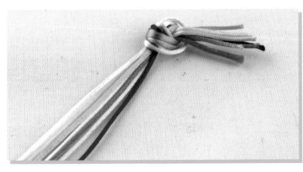

1 Place your seven 60cm (23½in) lengths of cord together, and knot them at one end.

2 Lower the knot into the centre of your disc.

3 Lay out the cords at numbers **32, 4, 8, 16, 20, 24** and **28**. Leave a gap at number **12**.

tip

Note where the gap is on the disc in relation to the cords you have laid out, as you will need to keep the gap in the same place after each move and every rotation of the disc, before filling the gap with the next move of your cord.

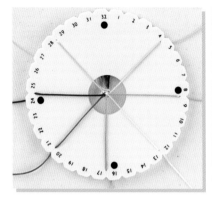

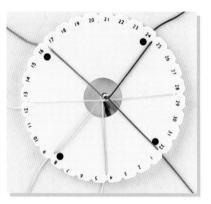

4 Move the cord from **32** to **12**.

5 Rotate the disc so that number **20** is at the top and the gap between the cords is in the same (four o'clock) position as shown in step 3.

6 Move the cord from **20** to **32**.

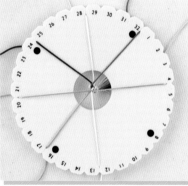

7 Rotate the disc so that the gap is in the same (four o'clock) position and number **8** is at the top of your disc.

8 Move the cord from **8** to **20**, then rotate the disc again so the gap is in the four o'clock position and number **28** is at the top of your disc.

The cord in progress.

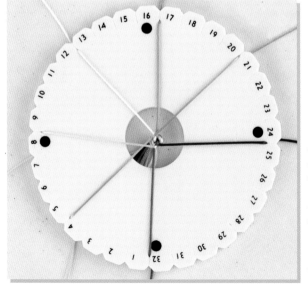

9 At this stage, to work out which cord to move into the gap next, count three cords back, anti-clockwise from the gap – this is the next cord that needs to move in to the gap.

Repeat steps 3 to 9, rotating the disc to keep the gap at four o'clock, then moving the cord sitting three numbers back from the gap anti-clockwise, to fill the gap each time. Repeat until your braid is at the desired length, then follow the instructions on pages 16–17 to remove the braid from the disc and attach the end caps.

JODIE

The completed seven-braid bracelet. Create your own variations in seven shades of one colour, or the seven colours of the rainbow.

MARKING UP A KUMIHIMO DISC

Rather than working with the numerals printed on the kumihimo disc, you may find it useful, before you even begin to load the disc and braid your cord, to turn over your disc and mark in pencil – or a pen with a fine point – the slots that you will be using.

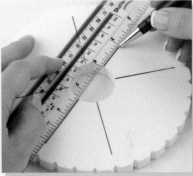

1 Using a ruler for precision, draw a pair of lines across the reverse of your disc, going from North to South.

2 Draw in a second pair of lines from West to East.

3 Count four slots between the first pairs of lines, and draw in two more pairs of lines.

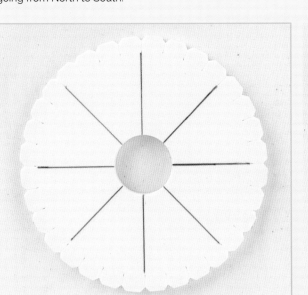

Your disc, with guidelines drawn on.

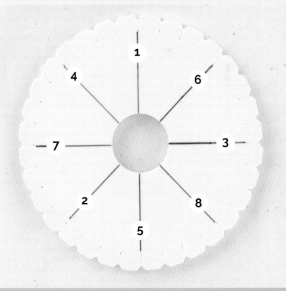

4 Number each of the lines as shown in the photograph above. Using this method, the first cord you move is at position **1**, down to position **8** (where the gap would have been). Then rotate the disc so number **2** is at the top, and then move the cord at **2** down to fill the gap at position **1**.

Continue to rotate your disc so that the next sequential number ends up at the top of the disc and the cord is moved from that number down to fill the gap.

Katie

Eight-braid square cord bracelet

This eight-braid project introduces a new repetition of moves that does not require you to rotate the kumihimo disc to braid a square cord. It does, however, require you to familiarize yourself with the initial positions of your cords on the disc, as you will return to these before beginning a new set of moves.

Use a smaller kumihimo disc for this project. The smaller diameter makes it easier for you to grip when you are holding the cord underneath.

You will need...

- Small kumihimo disc, 11cm (4¼in) diameter
- 3m (9ft) 2mm satin cord (white)
- 1m (3ft) 2mm satin cord (red)
- 6mm end caps

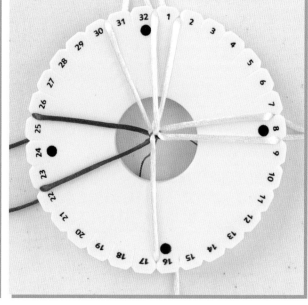

BEFORE YOU BEGIN

Cut three 1m (3¼ft) lengths of white cord, and one 1m (3¼ft) strand of red cord. Place the four strands together and tie them in the centre with 10cm (4in) surplus cord to form eight working cords.

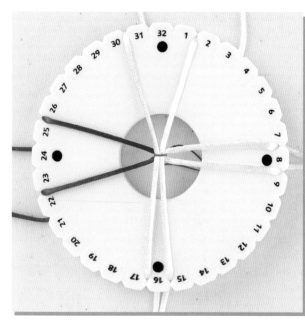

1 Arrange the cords on the disc. Place the white cords at numbers **30**, **1**, **7** and **8**, **15** and **16**. Place the red cords at numbers **22** and **25**.

2 Begin the braiding by taking the cord from **15** and moving it up to the right of **32**.

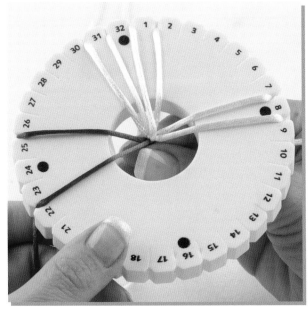

3 Take the cord from the right of **16** up to the right of **31**. Pull the braid down from underneath the disc to maintain the tension.

4 Take the cord from **1** down to **15**; then take the cord from **30** down to **16**. As you take the cords over, ensure the braid is still central in the middle of the disc.

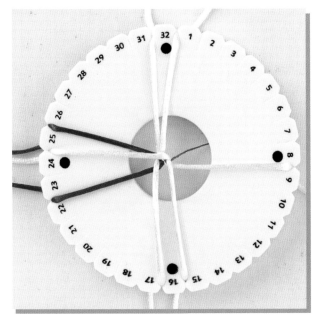

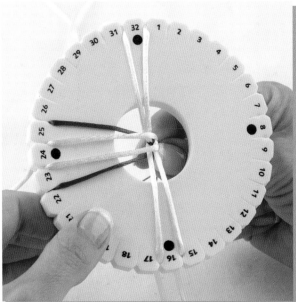

5 Take the cord from **7** over to **24**...

6 ...and the cord from **8** over to **23**. Pull down on the cord from the underside of the disc to stop the cords pulling too far over to the left side of the disc.

  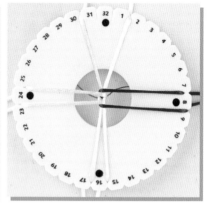

7 Take the cord from **25** over to **7**…

8 …and the cord from **22** over to **8**. Again, check that the braid is central in the middle of the disc.

9 Reposition the cords from **32** to **1** and **31** to **30**.

The next moves – to reposition the cords from **24** to **25**, and **23** to **22** – will bring your cords back to the same positions as shown in step 1, although the cord colours will be different.

Repeat the sequence from steps 1 to 9 until your braid reaches your desired length. Remove the braid from the disc and attach the end caps, following the instructions on pages 16–17.

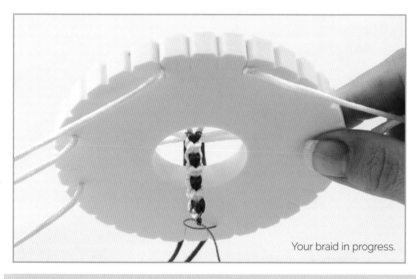

Your braid in progress.

COFFEE AND CREAM SQUARE CORD BRACELET

The coffee and cream square cord bracelet on the right is created by using two 1m (3¼ft) lengths of cream and two 1m (3¼ft) lengths of beige cord.

Lay the same colours opposite each other on the disc and braid following steps 1 to 9, above. This will create a stripe of each colour cord down your braid – as seen in the photograph on the opposite page.

KATIE

The completed square cord bracelets.

Melanie
Twelve-braid raised cord bracelet

This twelve-braid kumihimo project is a pretty, striped braid with a highlighted twist. Learn this new, simple repetition of moves without the need to rotate the disc.

You will need...

- Large kumihimo disc, 15cm (6in) diameter
- 2m (6½ft) 1mm satin cord (purple)
- 2m (6½ft) 1mm satin cord (pink)
- 3m (9¾ft) 1mm satin cord (white)
- 8mm end cap

tip

The cord you choose for the raised detail on this braid will use up to one and a half times the amount of cord compared with the other colours.

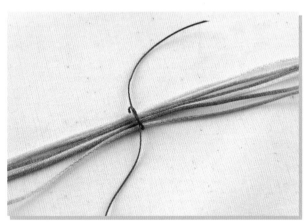

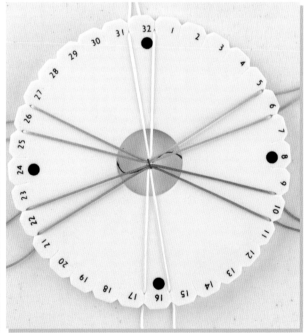

1 Cut the purple cord down to two 1m (3¼ft) lengths; cut the pink cord down to two 1m (3¼ft) lengths and the white cord down to two 1.5m (5ft) lengths. Place your six strands together and tie them in the centre with surplus cord (I have used blue cord, for contrast). Two of your strands will be longer than the others. You will now have twelve cords with which to braid.

2 Arrange your cords around the disc as shown above: the four, long strands of white cord – which will be your twisted, raised detail – should be to the right of **31**, **32**, **15** and **16**. The four purple strands sit to the right of **5**, **6**, **25** and **26**. The four pink strands sit to the right of **9**, **10**, **21** and **22**.

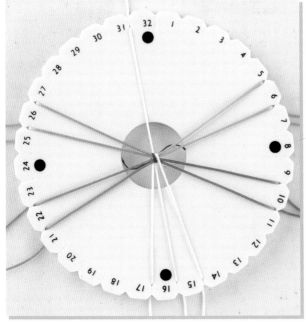

3 Move the white cord from **32** down to **14**.

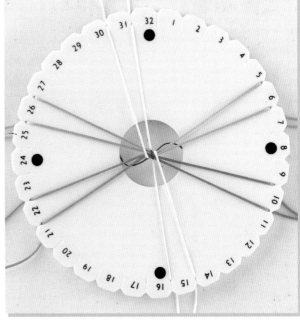

4 Move the cord from **16** up to **30**.

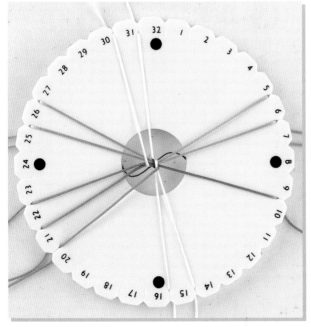

5 Move the pink cord all the way over from **10** to **20**.

tip

As you move the cord all the way across the disc at step 5, it will help to lift the cord upwards before you slot it into place (see the photograph below). This will ensure that you won't see the raised cord through the centre of your braid; it will also help the raised cord stand out when the braid is complete.

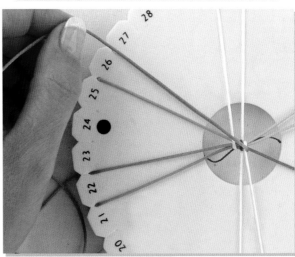

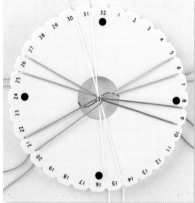 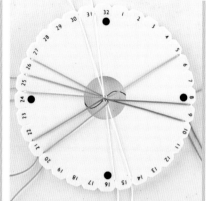 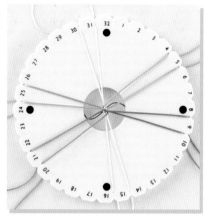

6 Take the cord from **22** over to **8** – this cord can go straight over; you do not need to lift up the cord before re-placing it.

7 Move the cord from **6** over to **24**.

8 Take the cord from **26** over to **4** – move this cord down towards the bottom of the disc before slotting it into place.

9 Repeat steps 3–8. Note that the numbers will rotate round the board so try to become familiar with the repetition of moves. The spacing between the braids will remain the same throughout the braid. As the braid starts to come through the centre, you may to twist it slightly in a clockwise direction to help position the threads and encourage the raised cord to stand out on the twist.

TO FINISH YOUR BRACELET

Continue to braid until your bracelet is the desired length, then finish your piece, following the instructions on pages 16–17.

MELANIE

The completed twelve-braid raised
cord bracelet.

INDEX